5TH GRADE GEOGRAPHY SEAS AND OCEANS OF THE WORLD

The sea or the ocean is a word used to describe all the interconnected salt waters of the world including the five great oceans.

Sea is used to name specific, smaller bodies of seawater. Seas usually make up partly landlocked areas within the much larger five great oceans.

Because of tidal and wind-driven changes, sea level is constantly fluctuating. Average sea level has risen between 10 cm and 25 cm in the past 100 years.

A mediterranean sea is a sea that is nearly completely enclosed by land and therefore has a very limited exchange of water with the outer oceans.

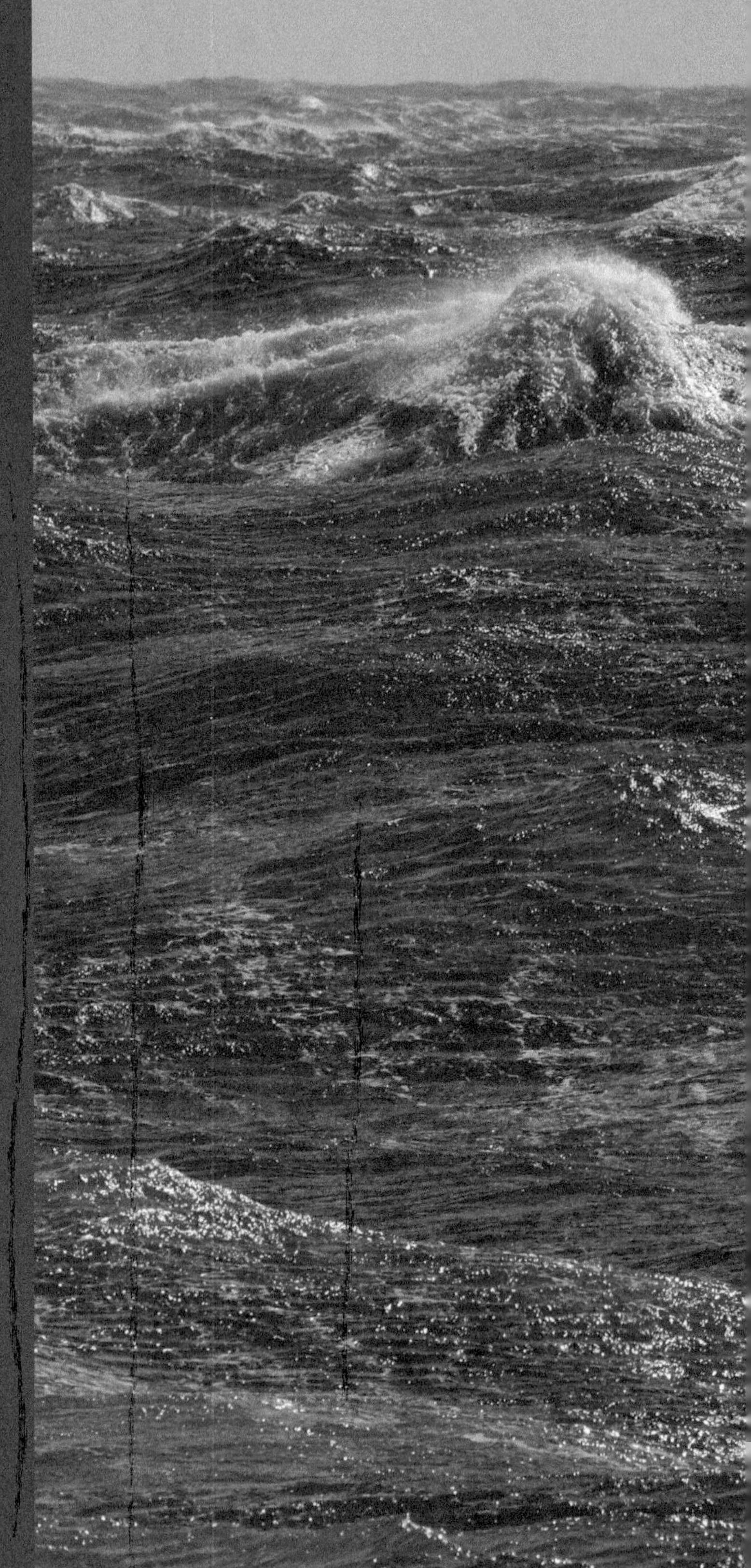
Around 70%
of the Earth's
surface is
covered by
oceans.

More than 90 percent of the planet's living biomass is found in the oceans.

The largest
ocean on Earth
is the Pacific
Ocean. It covers
around 30%
of the Earth's
surface.

The second
largest ocean
on Earth is the
Atlantic Ocean.
It covers over
21% of the
Earth's surface.